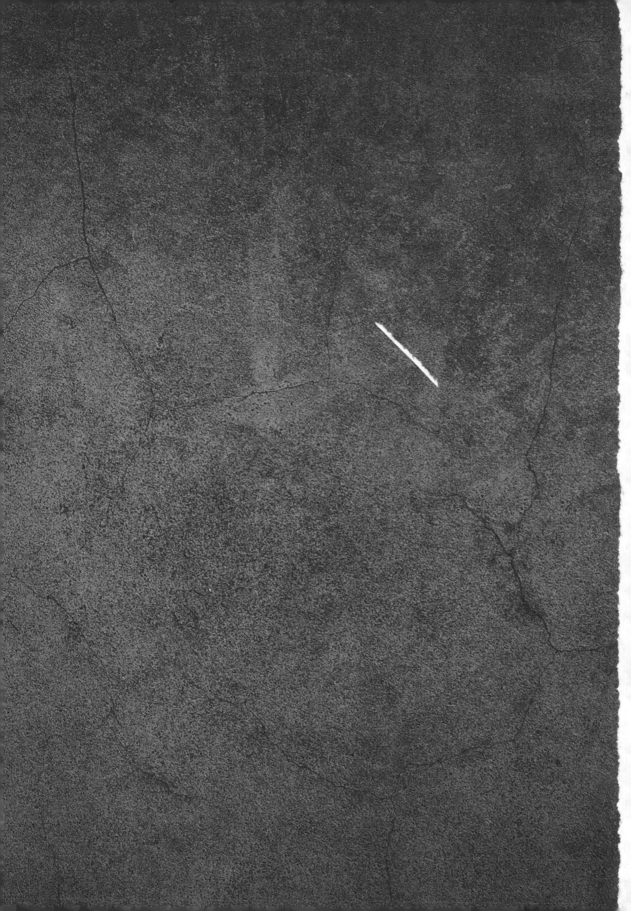

INUUNIRA

My Story of Survival

Published by Inhabit Media Inc.
www.inhabitmedia.com

Inhabit Media Inc. (Iqaluit) P.O. Box 11125, Iqaluit,
Nunavut, X0A 1H0

Design and layout copyright © 2022 Inhabit Media Inc.
Text copyright © 2022 Brian Koonoo
Illustrations by Ben Shannon copyright © 2022 Inhabit
Media Inc.

Editors: Neil Christopher and Anne Fullerton
Art Director: Danny Christopher

This project was made possible in part by the
Government of Canada.

We acknowledge the support of the Canada Council for
the Arts for our publishing program.

Library and Archives Canada Cataloguing in Publication

Title: Inuunira : my story of survival / by Brian
Koonoo.
Names: Koonoo, Brian, author.
Identifiers: Canadiana 20220209952 | ISBN 9781772274301
(hardcover)
Subjects: LCSH: Koonoo, Brian. | LCSH: Wilderness
survival—Canada, Northern. | LCSH: Survival—
    Canada, Northern. | LCSH: Traditional ecological
knowledge—Canada, Northern.
Classification: LCC GV200.5 .K66 2022 | DDC
613.6/909719—dc23

Printed in Canada

Canadä

Canada Council   Conseil des Arts
for the Arts   du Canada

INUUNIRA

My Story of Survival

by Brian Koonoo

illustrations by Ben Shannon

Contents

Inhabit Media Inc.

Part 1: A Hunter Is Born

I can remember being three years old, sitting between my father and the handlebars of his snowmobile, tracking through the snow. I would look at all the different landscapes that we passed, asking him what each place was called. Sitting on the snowmobile I would hum, and the sound of the snowmobile seemed to echo me, and I would eventually fall asleep. Sometimes as my head fell forward it would accidentally hit the emergency stop switch, and the snowmobile would lurch to a stop. So my father began to tie a rope around us both. This way I could sleep peacefully and wake up in a completely different area—sometimes to herds of caribou around us. I would watch in awe as my father hunted them.

One spring when I was young my family and I went on a camping trip to the floe edge of Baffin Bay. My father took me on the snowmobile to hunt *akpait*, murre. I sat steady on the seat of the snowmobile, and with my father's help, I tried aiming with the pump action .22 rifle. He told me, "You see this pointed thing at the end of the rifle? That's the front sight. Line it up with this rear sight on the other end and point it at the akpa. When you are ready, pull this trigger." I kept trying to aim for a long time. The bird kept moving, and I was having trouble lining up the sights and holding up the rifle. Finally, my father helped me aim. He said, "When I say *atii*, go, you pull the trigger." He aimed and said, "Atii." I pulled the trigger and the akpa quickly dropped into the water below. It sat and rapidly flapped its wings for a few seconds until it stopped moving altogether. I was overjoyed. My father said, "You shot your first animal." The akpa was too far out in the water to reach with a *niksik*, a gaff hook. So I pleaded with my father, and he agreed to unload the small aluminum boat we had brought with us from our *qamutiik* sled—it felt like it took forever, and I was anxious to retrieve my catch. Finally we took the boat into the water, and I got my akpa. I was all smiles after we got back on the ice. I examined my first catch and was thrilled that I could be like my father and be able to catch these animals. My father skinned it and said, "You'll have to eat it, it's your catch." I was so happy about my first catch that I wanted to keep it instead of eating it, so I stored it under our qamutiik. I went on with the day, watching the many birds flying by and zooming on the water peacefully. The next day I got up and my father told me, "I gave your akpa to your *ataatatsiaq*, your grandfather, so he could eat it." I asked him why, and he answered, "You weren't trying to eat it. It was going to spoil." This pained me at first, but I soon realized that at least my grandfather would eat my first catch, and I felt proud that I had fed someone. That was my first memory of hunting as a child, at age three.

Not long after that, my father was preparing to go caribou hunting. I wanted to go with him, but he said, "I am going very far, you will get cold." I started to cry so that he would take me with him, and he finally accepted my wish. My mother bundled me up in warm clothes, and we set off. We spent the night in a cabin, and the next day started our hunt. We came across a herd of caribou and he shot a few dead. But one was wounded and could not get up. We walked to it and my father loaded the rifle and pointed it at the neck of the caribou. He told me to pull the trigger. As soon as I pulled it, a loud bang went off, and it seemed as though the caribou got scared and tightened its muscles, flinching, and then died. I told my father, "*Tupaktualuk!*"—it got spooked! My father laughed and I could see his face fill with happiness, knowing that I would become a hunter. I had harvested my first caribou, and I was proud. I knew that one day I would be like my father, capable of travelling long distances and catching animals. That day, a hunter was engraved in me. A dream was planted to explore new places and catch animals.

Young Brian and Caribou

As I grew older, I continued to hunt every chance I had. When I turned thirteen, I started travelling alone to hunt. Once I went hunting for ptarmigan and Arctic hare ten kilometres away from my community. As I was going along a valley I spotted a hare and was able to shoot it. As I continued down the valley my snowmobile got stuck and flipped onto its side. I used all my strength trying to stand it back up and eventually got it going. As I travelled along the shore I got stuck again between two snowdrifts. This time I was completely stuck. It took me several hours to clear the snow under the snowmobile, but the machine still wouldn't budge. I was giving up, and I decided to kneel on the seat of the snowmobile and prayed aloud to God. Then I started the snowmobile, pulled the throttle, and amazingly it moved out of the drift and I was able to continue on my hunt. I cried with happiness, thanking the Lord for helping me out of my tough situation. I went onto the ice towards seal breathing holes that I remembered were nearby. When I got close to them I started hearing splashing sounds, and I knew the seals were pupping. I went to the nearby snowdrifts and checked for hollow areas under the snow. I found one and quickly started digging through the snow and ice. I saw a pup and hooked it quickly, before it had a chance to get down the breathing hole and back into the water. I had caught a seal and felt that I had truly become a hunter. I killed the seal pup and travelled back home, happy and proud, a smile on my face. I had harvested an Arctic hare and a seal pup on my own, and was also able to get my snowmobile out of the snow. I was amazed and thankful that after almost giving up I was able to get out, and on top of that, God had given me a seal pup to harvest.

As I became an adult, I had a wife and six lovely daughters to cherish and provide for. The will to provide them with healthy country food— traditional Inuit food—was ingrained in me. I would hunt seal, caribou, narwhal, polar bear, and other native animals. In the winter months I would go hunting alone, in the spring my family would sometimes come along, and for longer trips to hunt caribou I would often go with other hunters.

Pont Inlet, Nunavut

Caribou meat can be the most difficult to harvest, since there has been a shortage in our area. The winter of 2015 was one of the hardest because there was a caribou moratorium in place for Baffin Island. So we had to travel outside of the island to the mainland of Melville Peninsula to legally hunt caribou, which was about five hundred kilometres away.

I come from Pond Inlet, or Mittimatalik, a small community in the north of Baffin Island with a population of about 1,700. It's a small hamlet, like many others in the North, and a close-knit community. It's known as one of Canada's "Jewels of the North," with beautiful scenery and mountain ranges surrounding it. But I have always had the dream of travelling far away on a snowmobile to a place where I had never gone before. To journey to other communities and beyond was something I wanted to do ever since I started going hunting as a child with my father. A great opportunity came to fulfill this dream when I was thirty-six. I planned to travel to Igloolik to stay with my friend Perry, and beyond to the Naujaat region, where the caribou were. I would wait for spring, when there would be twenty-four-hour daylight, and I would set off.

Polar Bear

Pond Inlet, NU, to Naujaat, NU (Repulse Bay), approximately 500 KM

Part 2: Into the Tundra

May 10-11, 2015:

I left Pond Inlet on the longest caribou-hunting trip of my life. I was heading five hundred kilometres away to Naujaat, which was then called Repulse Bay. I had asked several people if they were willing to come with me, but none were, so I set off by myself. I knew a group of hunters had left the day before, and I planned to catch up with them.

My snowmobile was a Bombardier Expedition wide track 600 E-Tec. I made sure I did a full check on the snowmobile, ensuring everything was in good working order. I filled the snowmobile with gas and brought forty-five extra gallons, and two gallons of naphtha camping fuel. To carry everything I had my qamutiik, a twenty-foot-long, four-foot-wide sled that is pulled behind the snowmobile.

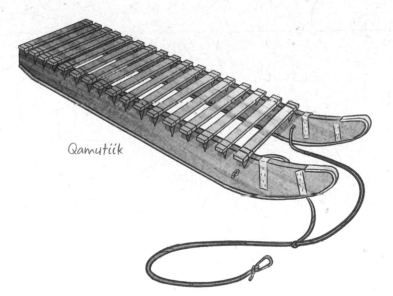

Qamutiik

I started packing my gear. Pond Inlet had recently received VHF radio repeaters, so I brought a VHF handheld radio that would allow me to communicate across shorter distances. I also brought a single sideband SBX-11A radio to communicate across longer distances, and a GPS for navigation. I also packed a four-person canvas tent, a sleeping bag and mattress, a backpack, a tarp, a tinned survival candle, a two-litre Thermos and one-litre Thermos mug, a cooler, a kettle, a Coleman stove, a .300 Sako rifle, a German butcher knife, and some Ziploc bags. I also brought my iPod so I could entertain myself with games and music. I brought enough food to last me a week, mainly coffee, tea, sugar, sandwich meat, and jerky. I dressed well in my sealskin wind pants, homemade winter parka, and sealskin mitts. I packed everything into my qamutiik, strapping a tarp over all my gear.

My first stop would be Igloolik, about three hundred kilometres away. I checked the weather, and it seemed reasonable to travel. Since our region was in twenty-four-hour daylight, darkness wouldn't be a problem. Everything was in order, so off I went—all alone, and with a huge determination and desire to explore a place where I had never gone before. I was living my dream.

Qamutiik and Snowmobile

Supply List

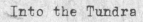

Mug

Plastic Bags

Rifle

Cooler

Butcher Knife

Sleeping Bag

Radio

Coleman Stove

Kettle

Packed Tent

Thermos

11

Just past Epiutalik, about one hundred kilometres from home, I saw a
lone snowmobiler stop ahead of me. I reached him and learned he was
a hunter who was travelling without a qamutiik. He had stopped to
fuel up his snowmobile from a five-gallon jerry can he had cached on a
previous trip. He said to me, "I am glad that you came by—there is no
funnel on this jerry can." I smiled and lent him mine. After he gassed up
I was off again.

I made it to the end of Milne Inlet to a hunter's cabin, five kilometres
east of the Baffinland Iron Mines loading port. I had a meal, topped
up my Thermos, and took a quick hour's rest. There was another two
hundred kilometres or so to reach Igloolik, and I was trying to catch up
with the other hunters, so I soon set off. The hunters I was following
had left a good trail to follow, so I had no problems navigating, and the
weather was good.

May 12:

I finally reached the sea ice at the edge of Igloolik. There was a bit of
drifting snow and whiteouts, and I lost the trail at times, but I managed
to find it again. In the distance I saw a bearded seal basking on the
ice. I thought that there must be a lot more bearded seals here, since
we never see them during this time of year near Pond Inlet. I thought I
would hunt the seal, but before I could get close it dove into its hole, so
I carried on. The wind and snow were picking up, so I travelled faster.
I was careful to avoid the dangers of melting streams, as it would be
easy to get stuck in slush—if I got wet, the freezing cold could lead to
hypothermia.

I reached Igloolik Island in the afternoon. The first things I spotted were
a few cabins, and as I continued on I saw an SUV in the distance.

I must be getting close, I thought. Before I knew it I saw the houses of Igloolik. I stopped on the shore, unhitched my qamutiik, and walked up to two people who were working on a snowmobile. They welcomed me to Igloolik and showed me the way to my friend Perry Atagootak's home. By the time I knocked on his door I was exhausted from the long trip and looking forward to sleep.

Perry and his wife greeted me, saying, "I can't believe you are already here! You make Pond Inlet seem very close." To me it felt very far, as I had travelled twenty hours to get there. Perry showed me the room I would be staying in and offered me some food and coffee. I called home and let my wife know that I had made it safely to Igloolik. I posted on Facebook to let my friends know as well, and while I was online I noticed that the hunters I was trying to catch up with were already in Hall Beach. Since I really needed the rest, I quickly fell asleep.

Snowdrifts

May 13:

The next day the weather was not ideal. The snow was drifting, but the visibility was fair, so I was comfortable leaving. I contacted a friend from Hall Beach, telling him I might stop by for coffee sometime in the afternoon. I gassed up the snowmobile, packed my gear, and left Igloolik. Anxious to get to where the caribou were, I travelled fast. I knew that the other hunters had already caught caribou and were camping between Hall Beach and Naujaat.

I couldn't use the stars and moon for navigation because of the twenty-four-hour daylight. The area was very flat compared to Pond Inlet, but luckily I could see the trail. There were *inuksuit* that made navigating easier. I also knew which way the wind was blowing, so I could follow the snowdrifts that were made by the wind. I also had the GPS that was connected to my snowmobile's power.

Inuksuk

Stopping halfway at an abandoned cabin to have coffee and a smoke, I soon reached Hall Beach and found my friend's house. I used the phone there to call home and notify my wife that I had made it safely. I told her I would continue towards Naujaat, where the caribou were, and hopefully meet up with the hunters from Pond Inlet. My wife said, "Okay, be careful." I answered, "Okay, I will. I love you," and hung up the phone. I had only used about fifteen gallons of gas from Pond Inlet—still enough gas to reach the caribou and return to Hall Beach, or go to Naujaat and get more gas. I soon left Hall Beach and continued on my journey, alone again.

I travelled through the evening until about midnight, when I came upon some hills and a small cabin. I stopped to camp for the night, but as I was unpacking I realized I had dropped my sideband radio, along with my sleeping bag. They had somehow slipped through the tarp on my qamutiik without me realizing it. I was angry—*why didn't I check my gear sooner?* With no communication, I could not notify my family where I was, and I had no clue where the group I was trying to reach were. I wondered if I should turn back or keep going. But I decided I couldn't turn back without catching any caribou after I had come so far, and I figured I was fairly close to other hunters. I pressed on towards Naujaat.

The day was cloudy with whiteouts and blizzards, and I used my GPS to navigate. I continued through the night, along valleys, and kept getting stuck on rocky terrain. I tried turning back to find a better route, but my snowmobile got stuck in deep snow. It took me hours to get it unstuck, only for it to get stuck again. I struggled for more hours until I was too exhausted to continue. I finally stopped and set up my canvas tent to camp for the night.

May 14:

I woke up with more energy and managed to get my snowmobile out of the snow. But as I started travelling, I noticed the snowmobile was having problems from the stress of the night before. I thought it was the drivebelt, so I replaced it. But the noises continued, coming from the front and underneath the track. I knew I was in trouble. I kept going, trying to get as close to Naujaat as possible—I was seventy-five kilometres away. The farther I got, the weaker the snowmobile became. I forced the machine along for as long as I could, hoping to make it to a community or at least a cabin before it gave out completely. But the machine couldn't go any farther—it ground to a halt, driving the qamutiik underneath the track and body of the snowmobile. The engine was still running, but it wouldn't go forward or backward. I tried to remove the qamutiik, but it was completely wedged in. I had no choice but to set up camp. Hopefully I would be rescued, but if not I would try to fix my snowmobile the next day and keep going.

GPS connected to the radio

Part 3: Lone Survival

May 15-16:

I woke up to a blizzard. Since I had no sleeping bag, I stayed in the tent with my Coleman stove on high to stay warm, only getting up to eat and drink hot coffee. The weather continued to be stormy and I was exhausted, so I stayed in the tent and slept for three days. Each day I hoped I would be found.

I had to try to communicate with someone to let them know where I was. I tried using my GPS, but the batteries had worn out. So I grabbed my VHF radio and climbed a hill beside my camp to try to connect with someone, but there was nothing. I tried burning garbage, but it didn't produce enough smoke for anyone to see from a distance. I went back to the tent to try to connect the radio battery to the GPS. I cut the external power cable of the GPS and connected it to the radio. It powered up and I got my location. I calculated my distance from Naujaat—I was sixty kilometres northwest of the community. I thought that if I could walk twenty kilometres a day I could make it there, or at least find people hunting near the area.

My camping fuel was running very low, so I had to get going. I packed up my tent, sleeping mattress, stove, and food onto the tarp and started walking, dragging my gear behind me. As I started walking through the deep snow, I soon realized the tarp was too heavy—if I continued that way, dragging it through snow and over rocks and hills, it would take too long and I would soon exhaust myself. After only a hundred metres I turned back to the snowmobile.

The weather had improved, so I knew I had to move quickly while I could. I decided to pack only what would fit in my backpack: my Thermos, the rest of the food I had, the survival candle, the knife, the rifle, the GPS, the radio, and a bunch of Ziploc bags. I tied the tarp to my backpack and started walking. I used the GPS that was now connected to the radio battery to get my location. I used the snowdrifts to keep walking straight for the direction of Naujaat.

How to Build an Iglu

You first must have the right type of snow, not too hard and not too soft, and enough of it to cut many blocks. You must think about the size first, and measure and mark the area where you will put up the blocks—you can tie a rope to a harpoon and use it to make a perfect circle. Then you start cutting up the blocks. This is not a simple job, as they need to be cut on an angle so the blocks are easier to pull out. As you stack the blocks, slant them towards you.

After cutting the angle, secure it with one pat on top and the block should stick like glue. Once you get to the final piece, cut the top like an oval following the other blocks. Once everything is done, make a door and go outside, and then start sealing the cracks with snow, using your knife to smooth it out.

Without a tent, I wondered how I was going to make shelter for myself. Although I knew how to make an *iglu*, there wasn't enough snow, and the condition of the snow wasn't right. But I remembered my father had once told me that if I was stuck in a storm and not able to build an iglu, I could use a knife to dig into a snowdrift just enough to lie down so I could get shelter and get warm from my body heat and breath. My father's words seemed loud and clear. He always said, "When I am gone, remember my words. Even if you forget, my words will come to you when you are going through tough experiences." I was touched by my father's wisdom, and I grew hopeful. I shouted, "I can do this! I will get myself out of this!" I thought, *If my ancestors survived for thousands of years with very little equipment, then I can survive as long as I'm eating and well hydrated.*

May 17:

The day I left the tent, the weather was holding up. The snow was fairly deep, and there were many hills and valleys to traverse. But I had energy and determination and was able to walk for about twenty-five kilometres, for twelve hours, until I was exhausted. The wind started to pick up, so I stopped to camp. I walked along a creek and came upon a large boulder where there was enough snow drifted beside it for me to dig into with my knife, removing the snow with my sealskin mittens. I crawled in, put the tarp under me, and closed the entrance with it. It was calm inside, so I had some food and a cup of coffee. But my clothes were soaked, so I knew I could not sleep long or I would freeze and likely never be found. I must have slept for only an hour, but I felt rested. I packed up and kept walking.

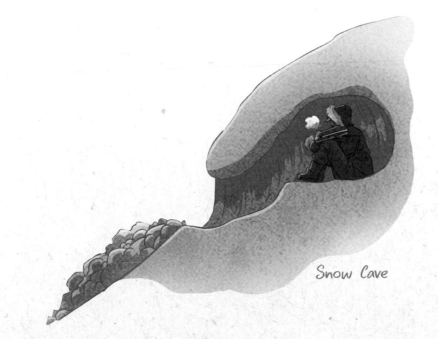

Snow Cave

I continued to walk, but the wind kept getting stronger and stronger, slowing me down. That night there was low visibility with whiteouts and drifting snow. I was walking into a valley, and as I couldn't clearly see the slope, I was going very slowly. Suddenly I heard a crack in front of me, so I quickly stepped back and lay down. The snow in front of me collapsed— there was a moment of silence, then a loud *swoosh*. The snow dropped about a hundred feet down. I started shaking. I was shocked that I hadn't fallen. I looked for another way down and managed to make it to the bottom safely. From there I looked up to where I had almost fallen. If I had been walking faster I would have been buried in the snow and never been found.

I continued walking until I couldn't go on any longer. I checked my GPS and saw that I had walked twenty kilometres—less than the day before. I found another large boulder and dug into the snowdrift beside it to sleep for the night. When I woke up my water was only lukewarm, and getting colder by the moment. I only took a small sip.

May 18:

I left the cave and emerged into the freezing cold and drifting snow.
I took my backpack and started walking, but I was still exhausted
and could only walk about a hundred metres at a time before I would
collapse in the deep snow. I could see in the distance a herd of caribou.
Every time I fell the herd stopped and looked at me. I thought about
shooting one, but I still had some food and didn't want to waste a whole
animal. The herd came closer and closer to me as I walked, so close that
I started to talk to them. I asked, "Do you know where Naujaat is? Can
I hop on to Naujaat?" They came back to me three times, and it was the
closest I have ever been to caribou.

I started seeing Twin Otter planes taking off from the direction of
Naujaat and thought there must be a military exercise going on. I didn't
think there would be people searching for me. But many thoughts did
start to run through my head. How my family must be worried about
me. And about my ancestors, how they managed to survive in very cold
temperatures with very little gear. I was proud of my ancestors, and this
gave me hope. *I am an Inuk*, I thought. *I know that I can survive.* And I
kept going.

But as I kept walking I was getting weaker and weaker. I finished some
sandwich meat I still had and the last of the water from my Thermos. I
thought about how I could get more water and remembered what my
father had taught me. He had showed me how to make three concave
hollows in ice, from biggest to smallest, then to set a flame in the biggest
hollow, and melted water would start to flow to the one below it. The
water at the bottom would be pure enough to drink. But the wind was
too strong for this to work. I walked on, climbing hill after hill, hoping
to find a cabin over the next one. I started to pray, "Please God, get me a

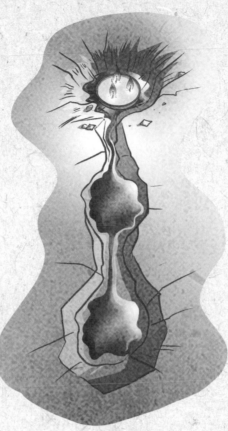

Hollows in Ice

cabin." But every time I reached the top of a hill, all I could see were more hills. I started shouting, "Naujaat! Naujaat!" I continued walking into the rising wind.

I came to an area that was mostly gravel, with hardly any snow to be seen. I was exhausted and needed to find somewhere to camp. I would climb a hill and think I spotted a cabin, getting closer and closer until I realized it was a boulder, not a cabin. My eyes were playing tricks on me. The wind was getting worse and worse, and I was getting worried. I thought of my family, of my ancestors. I remembered a time when I was a member of the search and rescue and we were searching for a thirteen-year-old boy who was lost in a blizzard. We searched for three days but couldn't find him. Three days later he was found frozen. I fell to the ground thinking of that boy, how he died alone. I couldn't help myself but cry.

This reminded me of the time my father was four and he and his family almost froze and starved. Someone had taken their dogs, saying they had to go check their cache and would be right back, but they never returned. They left my father and his parents with no dogs, and no choice but to travel a hundred kilometres by foot, making *igluit* along the way. My grandfather eventually managed to catch a seal, but he was so hungry and exhausted by this point that as he was pulling it up he almost fainted and froze. But he made it back to the iglu to warm up and rest. He went back for the seal, pulling it behind him, falling in the snow and losing consciousness on the way back. But he continued on, and every time he got up he could see that the iglu was closer, as if an angel was carrying him nearer. He made it to the iglu, my grandmother prepared the seal, and they were able to survive from it. I thought of my grandfather as I slowly started falling asleep. I wished an angel would lift me up, or a spirit would bring me closer to my destination. Every time I got up I checked my GPS, but I hadn't moved. I would cry, "Why isn't a spirit, why isn't God, helping me?"

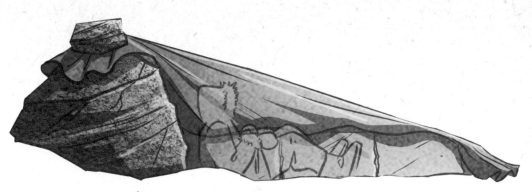

Tarp Enclosure

I kept walking slowly, growing more exhausted, with no more water, and no snow in sight to make a camp. Eventually I found a rock about two feet high with a small snowdrift around it. I cut up blocks of the snowdrift, put my tarp over the rock, and put the snow blocks on top of the tarp. I saw a rock about fifty metres away and barely managed to lift it onto my knees and make it back to the tarp. I put it on the tarp so it wouldn't blow away. I crawled underneath, took out Ziploc bags, and placed them on the snow to serve as a bed so I wouldn't get soaked by lying on the snow.

I was feeling very weak, so I ate a mouthful of sugar, quickly regaining my strength. I took out the survival candle I had and lit its three wicks. I took the lid and filled it with snow, holding it over the flames and waiting for the snow to melt. My hands were shaking with cold and exhaustion, and I had to be careful not to spill or let the flames go out. It seemed to take forever. Finally the water started boiling and I took a small sip of hot water.

I ate some more sandwich meat. I was worried about freezing in the night, so I pulled my arms through the sleeves of my parka like it was a sleeping bag. I snuggled in my parka and was getting nice and warm, praying that I would stay warm throughout the night. I slept for about five hours.

May 19:

When I woke up I stepped outside into howling wind and drifting snow. I got very cold very fast, since my clothes were damp from breathing in them while I slept. I started panicking. I thought, *If I don't start moving I'm going to die.* So I quickly packed my things into my backpack, but when I tried to zipper it shut, the zipper broke. I started to panic. I would have to bring even less gear. I was shivering, afraid I would die of hypothermia. I could feel my clothes freezing instantly, and it was becoming hard to move. My mind was racing. I felt the need to start walking right away to warm up.

So I took just my rifle, knife, GPS, radio, tarp, and Ziploc bags. I kept moving.

I knew I had to find a way to get drinking water. I remembered a survival skill I was once taught by an Elder. They had taught me to catch a rabbit, take the innards out, and place some snow in Ziploc bags in the cavity. The snow would melt and I'd have drinking water. If I had a fire I could even cook the rabbit, and the water would become broth. But there were no signs of rabbits anywhere. Then I remembered my father saying that when they were starving his grandmother would put a metal cup on her belly to melt ice to give my father something to drink. So I filled some Ziploc bags with snow and put them inside my parka to melt. I was proud to be experiencing something my ancestors also experienced.

I knew if I didn't keep moving I would get hypothermia, lose the strength to walk, and die of exposure. So I kept walking, but I could only go about fifty metres before I would get exhausted and have to stop. I'd cover myself with the tarp and rest before trying again. The blizzard continued. But when I got up once more the tarp blew away. I tried running after it, but the wind was strong. I was watching the tarp blow away and wishing I was being blown away too.

I kept getting up, walking, falling, and I was close to giving up. I started crying and losing hope. I fell on my back and looked up at the clouds. One looked exactly like an angel with a trumpet and wings, and I knew that people were praying for me. A thought came to me—there must be a reason I was going through this. There must be something I have to show people. That we Inuit can survive. We have very strong ancestors who survived in the harshest of environments. They made use of everything, and made it through periods of starvation. We are here today because of their struggles, and we owe a huge amount of respect to them. I started thinking of how easy life had become and what we take for granted—we just turn on the tap to get water. Put the thermostat up to get warmer. Flip a switch for light. Can easily contact someone from the other side of the world. But learning the survival skills and Inuit way of life is still very important. If the time comes, having these skills could be the difference between life and death. Knowing how to make shelter and how to get water and food can change your life.

I then thought of all the people I knew who had committed suicide. Most of them were in my community, with good shelter, food, and running water. But they had given up on life because of the struggles they had that they could not talk about. Suicide doesn't take away the pain; it passes it on to loved ones. If they had only realized that the troubles wouldn't always be there, that the pain and struggle may become a lesson to provide strength in difficult times. Life is precious. I had to share the message with others not to give up. No matter what happens.

So I got up and I continued walking. My legs started to cramp and I couldn't continue without limping, stopping to stretch so that I could carry on. I carried on like that all day, walking very slowly, tumbling down, falling forward, falling back. I fell again, losing my will to survive. I started crying, and my teardrops were freezing my eyes shut.

I shouted, "Please God, give me strength!" Minutes later I got more energy and continued on. I started coming upon small canyons, climbing one after another. I became overwhelmed and fell down, depleted. I fell asleep, and must have slept for half an hour. Then I could hear my kids saying, "Ataata, Ataata"—Father, Father. They were trying to wake me up. The thought of my daughters kept me going.

I then heard a sound. I looked up and saw Hercules planes and thought maybe they were searching for me. As they flew by I waved my arms

Hercules Plane

frantically, and I tried to reflect my knife with the sun to get the attention of the pilots, but they never spotted me. I kept walking, and the wind kept blowing. I tried using my radio to call emergency channels, *mayday!*, but there was no answer. I became frustrated and started shouting, "I am down here!" But the planes just continued on.

I walked another kilometre but fell backward on the snow again and fell asleep. The sound of a ptarmigan calling "*Avvaaq! Avvaaq!*" woke me. At first it was quiet and I was falling back to sleep, but it was getting louder and louder, and it sounded like it was urging me on. "Okay, I'll get up!" I answered. I now had more energy to walk, but I soon became tired again, and I fell forward. I looked at the snow right under my eyes, and in block letters I saw writing on the snow: "DKIDS." I was puzzled and thought I was hallucinating, so I wiped my eyes, but it was still there. As I touched the letter "S," the wind started to blow the letters away. Something was telling me to keep going and remember my kids. I thought of my daughters and started crying. I wanted to see them again. So I summoned all my strength, got up, and continued on.

I came across rocks and sat to rest. I noticed that there was snow melt on the bedrock, forming puddles under the ice. I crawled to it and chipped the ice with my knife, and there was water underneath! I drank the water, so thankful, calling, "Ataata!" I didn't stay long—the water gave me energy and I continued walking. I wanted to listen to music, but my iPod had run out of batteries long ago. So I sang songs I made up, and some I knew. My spirits lifted. I came to valleys and knew I was getting closer to Naujaat. I spotted inuksuit and followed them—they would show me the right path.

I finally made it to the sea ice of Naujaat. Between me and the ice was a large, deep crack. Although there was no open water, I could easily fall in and not be able to climb back out. But I leaped with all my strength and was able to make it safely onto the ice. As I walked on the ice, the wind was picking up. I was losing all my energy and fell on the ice to rest. I was falling asleep quickly, but when I looked up I saw ravens circling me, like vultures. They started dogging towards me as if they were trying to attack. I didn't know if they thought I was dead or were urging me on.

I looked up and couldn't believe what I saw at the top of the next hill—there was a cabin. I had made it to a cabin alive! I felt so relieved, knowing I would be sheltered from the wind—knowing that I would survive. I made it up the hill and to the porch, but the cabin was boarded up and locked. I found two hammers behind the cabin and used them to pry open the lock. When I got inside I filled a kettle with water and started the propane stove right away. I took my outdoor clothing off, as it was soaked. I drank coffee. There wasn't much food around, but I found a vegetable soup package and ate that. The wind started to pick up so much that the cabin was shaking. There was an HF and a CB radio in the cabin, but I could only hear static. I checked my GPS and saw that I was only three kilometres from Naujaat. I was so exhausted that I stayed to rest and dry my clothes. It was nice and warm in the cabin, and I slept for twelve hours.

May 20:

When I woke up there was still a blizzard—so much snow had blown in that I could hardly budge open the door. I had tea and looked for more food. There was only lard, flour, and baking powder, so I ate some of the lard and set out to walk to the town. The wind was blowing behind me, pushing me towards the community.

Brian Returns Home

Part 4: Sanctuary

I finally saw the community of Naujaat and walked to the nearest house. I approached the house and reached out and touched it—it was too good to be true. "Thank you, God, I made it!" I said, crying with relief. It was 5:30 a.m. I saw down the street a house with a taxi parked outside it and thought they might be awake, so I went there and knocked on the door. There was no answer, so I tuned the doorknob and the door opened. I could see a lady sleeping on the couch, so I said, "Hi, I broke down and I walked here." She got very excited and asked, "Are you the one they are looking for?" I told her I must be, and she told me her husband was helping with the search and went to get him. He was so amazed I had found my way safely, and offered me food and drinks right away. I only wanted a cigarette and to use the phone.

My mother was the first to answer her phone. She was so surprised, like she thought she was never going to hear from me again. Soon after I was able to reach my wife and children. We were so glad to hear one another that we mostly cried. I told them I was fine and would be home soon. I then called my co-worker who lived in the area to let him know I was all right. He came over right away and we hugged and cried as soon as he walked in.

We went to his house, and his family welcomed me and we ate breakfast. I was so relieved that I had survived my ordeal. Elders started to arrive even though it was very early in the morning. They must have heard about my journey on the morning news.

May 21-25:

I stayed and recovered for the next day.

Then a hunter offered to help me go recover my snowmobile and gear. It took us six hours to reach the campsite. We loaded everything and towed it back to Naujaat. Over the next few days I tried to repair my snowmobile, but there was too much damage. I was lucky enough that there was a good second-hand one for sale nearby. With the help of relatives and my community I was able to purchase it, and I was soon ready to leave. I am honoured that the community of Naujaat held a community feast for me before I left.

May 26-31:

I started my trip home, alone again. On the way back I spotted a familiar herd of caribou. I thought, *These are the same caribou I spoke to on my journey.* I caught three of the caribou near Naujaat, skinning them and putting them on my qamutiik. I came across a family who were fishing on a lake, and they told me there were hunters heading to Igloolik who were at a camp farther ahead, so I went to catch up with them and found the cabin. I fell asleep there and woke to snoring—the cabin was full of the hunters. We took off together and I killed another two caribou, skinning them and putting them on the qamutiik with the others.

We passed Hall Beach and arrived to Igloolik, where I stopped to see Perry. By now it was the end of May, and he told me that the snow was melting fast on Baffin Island. I had to rush to get back. Perry said, "I'll come with you, make sure you're not alone." When we got to the Baffin Island side we started going through very rocky areas, and I kept getting stuck. The runners in the sled were wearing out, and I was almost wearing out too. But we fixed the runners, and luckily two search-and-rescue members from Pond Inlet were able to help us get back home.

I was so happy when I made it onto the ice near home. I was going to make it. I felt like dancing on the sea ice. But by this time we were all very low on gas. We came to Epiutalik, the same location where I had stopped to share my funnel with the hunter. There was another jerry can there just as I was running out of gas. I thought, *What a coincidence*. Then I started thinking, *I wonder if that hunter was real, or if he was a* tarriaksuq—*a shadow person*. It would have been rare for someone to be travelling out that far without a sled. I had helped him out in that area, and it seemed that he was helping me out now in return.

Bylot Island

Finally I saw the mountains of Bylot Island. I knew I had made it home, and that I was going to see my family again. When we arrived to the ice in front of town, there was a crowd of people there to welcome me. When I saw my children and my wife I could not hold back my tears, crying as I drove closer. My family was crying and laughing. I was so thankful to everyone, but felt sorry for letting them worry. I felt overwhelming support and realized that my life is special and I am loved. I was so joyful to see my family again—after almost thinking that I never would.

Qajaq

Narwhals

Part 5: The Ongoing Journey

I knew that my traditional knowledge was what helped me survive. I was proud to have gone through similar struggles as my ancestors. And my journey of survival did not deter me, but made me all the more eager to continue hunting. I have always thought that Inuit should continue traditional ways of hunting—like catching narwhal with an *unaaq*, a harpoon.

The summer following my journey of survival, I practised using a *qajaq*, a kayak, and took it to the sea to catch narwhal. I threw the *avataaq*, the float, into the water as soon as I struck the whale with the unaaq, but the drag got caught on the qajaq. The qajaq capsized and I fell into the water. Luckily I was wearing a flotation device. I swam away but returned to the qajaq when the spear head came off the narwhal. I tried turning the qajaq upright, but it kept tipping over, so I waited to be rescued. A canoe came and pulled me out of the water and I just smiled—it was a lot of fun. I want to continue hunting narwhal in this way, and encourage others to do the same.

During that winter of 2015, the people of Pond Inlet were not able to catch many narwhal, so they weren't able to make much *maktaaq*, whale blubber. When the sea froze over, someone was able to hear narwhal with a hydrophone, which is a device that is able to hear sounds underwater. So we created a search party and looked for the whales full-time for over two weeks. After looking for so long, the search party was on the verge of giving up; so was I. Eventually I went off on my own to search and became distracted by a raven flying and calling. I followed it until I saw polar bear tracks. I stopped and listened with my ears, hearing calling sounds from under the water. As I approached the sound, it grew louder and louder. I started to shake—I had found the whales! I called on my VHF radio and asked the search party to come. They couldn't believe I had found the narwhal. And it was just in time—they were being imprisoned in the ice as their breathing hole was freezing over. We kept the ice from freezing over with ice chisels and harpoons. The people had me kill the first whale because I had been the one to find them, so I had first choice. My wife caught one, and so did my oldest daughter. Everyone was thankful that I had survived so that I could help my people.

My journey of survival gave me the opportunity to help my people. And it also taught me many things that I can share. Whenever you are experiencing difficult circumstances, remember that we have ancestors who were strong people. They were able to survive the most difficult conditions. Education is important, and learning traditions and survival skills is also important. We must work to strengthen Inuit culture and skills. We have to make sure that the future generations do not lose our way of life. Inuit are strong, and they are stronger when they help each other.

Glossary of Inuktut Words

Inuktut is the word for Inuit languages spoken in Canada, including Inuktitut and Inuinnaqtun. The pronunciation guides in this book are intended to support non-Inuktut speakers in their reading of Inuktut words. These pronunciations are not exact representations of how the words are pronounced by Inuktut speakers.

For more resources on how to pronounce Inuktut words, visit inhabitmedia.com/inuitnipingit.

Word	Pronunciation	Definition
akpait	AHK-pah-eet	murres (three or more)
ataata	ah-TAH-tah	father
ataatatsiaq	ah-TAH-taht-see-ahk	grandfather
atii	ah-TEE	go
avataaq	ah-vah-TAHK	float
iglu	EE-gloo	snow house
igluit	EE-gloo-eet	snow houses (three or more)
inuksuit	ee-NOOK-soo-eet	plural of inuksuk
inuksuk	ee-NOOK-sook	rock cairn used to aid hunters and indicate direction
inuunira	ee-NOO-nee-rah	how I'm alive
maktaaq	mahk-TAHK	narwhal or beluga skin and blubber
niksik	NEEK-sik	gaff hook
qajaq	KAH-yahk	kayak
qamutiik	KAH-moo-teek	sled
tarriaksuk	tah-ree-AHK-sook	shadow person
tupaktualuk	too-PAHK-too-ah-look	it got spooked
unaaq	oo-NAHK	harpoon

Contributors

Brian Koonoo

Brian Koonoo was born and grew up in Pond Inlet. He is married to Samantha Koonoo, originally from Rankin Inlet. They have six daughters at home: Chantal, Janelle, Josephina, Shanelle, Alina, and Alaira. Chantal and her partner Curtis have a son named Rogan, who is Brian and Samantha's first grandson and the first boy in the family. Brian currently works with Parks Canada as a resource management officer. Brian continues to hunt and provides country food for his family, relatives, and community.

Ben Shannon

Ben Shannon is a Canadian-born award-winning illustrator, animator, and father of two. An alumni of Sheridan College's Illustration program, Ben has worked for numerous high-profile clients, including *National Geographic, Rolling Stone, The Globe and Mail, The Wall Street Journal,* Nike, Universal Music, Marvel, and DC Comics. Winner of the Advertising and Design Club of Canada Interactive Design Illustration Award in 2008 and the Applied Arts award of excellence in the field of illustration in 1998, his work was also nominated for a Canadian Screen Award in 2014.

Photo Credits

Front cover: "Young Brian" by Koonoo family; "Brian's Face" by Brian Koonoo; "Brian on Tundra" by JaySimon Nashook; "Snowmobile" by Jedidah Merkosak; "Brian's Late Father Joseph Telling Brian's Nephews to Watch and Learn" by Koonoo family; "Polar Bear" by Brian Koonoo; "Handwritten Notes" by Brian Koonoo; "98809472" by AleksandrN/Shutterstock; "1538686316" by GROGL/Shutterstock; "1107092960" by Pam Walker/Shutterstock. Back cover: "Brian and Narwhal" by Samantha Koonoo. Table of contents: "Brian and his Mother Rhoda" by Koonoo family; "Brian Returns 1" by Jedidah Merkosak; "158385842" by RG-vc/Shutterstock. Page 2: "Young Brian" by Koonoo family; "Koonoo Camping" by Koonoo family; "Young Brian and Snowmobile" by Koonoo family. Page 5: "Young Brian and Caribou" by Koonoo family. Page 6: "704607751" by Exclusive Aerials/Shutterstock. Page 7: "Polar Bear" by Brian Koonoo. Page 8: "227398408" by Sergiy Bykhunenko/Shutterstock. Page 13: "Inuit use 'Uqalurait' to navigate" by Shari Fox, National Snow and Ice Data Center, https://www.flickr.com/photos/nsidc/50269268747. Page 30: "Brian Returns 2" by Jedidah Merkosak; "Snowmobile" by Jedidah Merkosak. Page 33: "1538557427" by GROGL/Shutterstock. End sheets: "1708695829" by mrmohock/Shutterstock.

INHABIT
MEDIA
Iqaluit • Toronto